Tlingit Wood Carving

TLINGIT WOOD CARVING SERIES

VOLUME 1
How to Carve a Tlingit Tray

VOLUME 2
How to Carve a Tlingit Hat

VOLUME 3
How to Carve a Tlingit Mask

Tlingit Wood Carving

How to Carve a Tlingit Tray

RICHARD A. BEASLEY *(Dee<u>x</u>wudu.oo)*

Foreword by ROSITA WORL *(Yeidiklas'o<u>k</u>w; <u>K</u>aa hani)*

Project Essays by KATHY MILLER *(Teet Tláa)*

Edited by KATHY DYE *(K'ei Joon)*

Principal Photography by MARK KELLEY

Published by SEALASKA HERITAGE INSTITUTE, Juneau, Alaska

SEALASKA HERITAGE INSTITUTE
One Sealaska Plaza, Suite 301
Juneau, Alaska 99801
907.463.4844
www.sealaskaheritage.org

The preparation of this volume was made possible in
part by a grant from the U.S. Department of Health
and Human Services, Administration for Children
and Families, Administration for Native Americans,
Social and Economic Development Strategies (SEDS)
program.

Library of Congress Control Number: 2009939605
ISBN 978-0-9825786-0-5

Design and composition by Kathy Dye.
Tlingit words edited by David Katzeek and Linda
Belarde with additional assistance from Nora and
Richard Dauenhauer, Keri Edwards, Hans Chester,
and John Martin.
Printed by Create Space, Scotts Valley, CA, U.S.A.

PHOTO CREDITS
All photographs in this book were made by Mark
Kelley, except the following: Men in Hoonah wear-
ing their clan's *at.óowu*, William Paul, Jr., Collection,
courtesy of Ben Paul, page viii; Old totem at Chief
Shakes Tribal House, Linn A. Forrest Collection at
Sealaska Heritage Institute, page ix; Chief Shakes
Tribal House, Linn A. Forrest Collection at Sealaska
Heritage Institute, page x; Opening night of the Juried
Art Show and Competition, photo by Brian Wallace,
page xi; Southeast Alaska, photo by Todd Antioquia,
page xii; Tlingit tools, photos by Kathy Dye, pages 2
and 5; Man's lidded toolbox and contents, Princeton
University Art Museum, lent by the Department of
Geology and Geophysical Sciences, Princeton University PU 5202, photo by Steve Henrikson, page 4;
Carved Tlingit dish, Alaska State Museum, Juneau
ll-B-814, photo by Sara Boesser, page 8; Tlingit feast
tray, photos by Kathy Dye, page 9; Tlingit War Helmet, photo by Fairfield Auction, LLC, page 34; Tlingit
paint pigments and eggs, photo by Kathy Dye and
Donald Gregory, page 35.

Front cover: Excerpt from *Legend of the Raven and
the Whale* by Richard A. Beasley (*Deexwudu.oo*). An
illustration of a story owned by the Coho (*L'uknax.
ádi*) Clan.

Contents

Traditional and Contemporary Art:
A Vehicle of Cultural Survival and Innovation

When Westerners first arrived on the Northwest Coast of North America, they found a distinctive art tradition that had developed over several thousand years. The art forms were unlike any other indigenous artistic tradition they had encountered anywhere else in the world. Among the Tlingit and Haida of Southeast Alaska, art adorned everything, from their houses, utilitarian objects and equipment, and clothing to their ceremonial objects.

While the indigenous artists appreciated the aesthetics of their works of art, and artisans held a special place in their society, the Tlingit and Haida had no word in their vocabulary that translated into art or artist as it is understood in the Western world.

The significance of Tlingit and Haida art lies in the social and ceremonial sphere of their lives. Although their art depicts beings and features of the natural world, they actually symbolize the spiritual dimensions of these beings and natural features. *Art is imbued with sacredness.* It reflects the spiritual relationship between humans and the beings depicted on the physical objects as well as their ongoing and perpetual relationship with their ancestors. It also identifies the social affiliation of individuals as members of a clan or house. During their ceremonies, the spiritual and natural worlds intersect through the use and display of their ceremonial objects that are identified as *haa at.óowu* or a clan's sacred property. It is a unique artistic tradition that developed over thousands of

Opposite: Brown Bear (*Teikweidí*) Clan hat, *at.óow* of the *Teikweidí* of Angoon. Published with permission from Jennie Jim, *Teikweidí* House Mother of Angoon.

vii

Men in Hoonah wearing their clan's *at.óowu.*

years and that holds a prominent place in the lives of the Tlingit and Haida people.

Ironically, both the flourishing of Northwest Coast art as well as its deterioration have been attributed to influences from Western societies. These ethnocentric assertions, however, ignore the complexities of sociocultural change and fail to acknowledge the role that Natives played in these changes. Natives are simply cast as passive recipients of culture change. Art historians have credited the refinement and surge in Northwest Coast art to the introduction of metal tools and wealth brought by Euro American traders and explorers who frequented the Northwest coastal areas beginning in the mid 1700s. Metal tools allowed for greater precision and increased production of finer art. It has been suggested by those who have written about Northwest Coast art that contact with Westerners and the trading opportunities they brought facilitated a greater accumulation of wealth that allowed the Tlingit to sponsor an increased number of ceremonies and to produce more ceremonial art.

The deterioration and decline in Tlingit art production began after the Americans assumed jurisdiction of Alaska in 1867. The missionaries joined forces with the military and civil authorities to suppress the traditional belief systems and practices. These immigrants to Alaska denounced Native art as a manifestation of pagan religions. Some missionaries even erroneously believed that the Tlingit worshipped the totemic beings depicted on their art work. Although the potlatch was never formally banned in Alaska as it was in Canada, the coercive actions of both missionaries and civil authorities had the same effect of curtailing ceremonial life and driving the ceremonies underground. Additionally, these newcomers, who believed in the superiority of their ways and beliefs, implemented policies to transform the "savage" Tlingit and Haida into brown, civilized, Christian citizens.

Although the production of traditional art was never fully eradicated, the pedagogical, ceremonial, social, and economic systems that had supported the creation and development of one of the most complex and sophisticated forms of indigenous art traditions all but disappeared. The rituals initiating the young aspiring artists into the profession and stimulating their latent creative talents were abandoned. The rigorous apprentice system in which young men and women spent years training under master artisans and learning the complex rules and forms of Northwest Coast art was also abandoned. Young artists no longer had the advantage of seeing or studying the older and aesthetically finer pieces that had been expropriated by a round of collectors who frequented the villages.

Additionally, the series of ceremonies associated with the commissioning of new works and procuring and preparing the natural resources for their transformation into art were also abolished under the new Western regimes that saw no value in the traditions and practices of the Tlingit. The social exchange between Eagle and Raven clans, in which artists of the opposite clan are commissioned to make a clan's *at.óowu*, was seriously weakened. The traditional system that supported the production of art and that was as complex and structured as the art form itself, collapsed.

Old totem poles at Chief Shakes Tribal House in Wrangell, Alaska. Photo collected circa 1915.

Art historians have tended to ignore or underscore the Westerners' suppression of the system that gave rise to Northwest Coast art as a causal factor in the deterioration of Native art. Furthermore, they uniformly proclaim that the effervescence or the Golden Age of Northwest Coast art can be attributed to the arrival of Westerners with their new tools and technology they brought and the wealth they generated. These writers further fail to acknowledge or understand the complexity of cultural change and innovations, and the resilience of ancient Tlingit beliefs and practices that contributed to the survival of Native art in the face of suppressive actions by the Americans.

Some art objects that were replaced by Western technology and material disappeared from Tlingit and Haida societies. For ex-

Ceremony at the Chief Shakes Tribal House in Wrangell. The totem poles were restored and the house rebuilt through a public work project funded by the Civilian Conservation Corps during the Great Depression.

ample, canoes and utilitarian objects such as those made of basketry and textiles were replaced by commercially manufactured boats and utilitarian objects and clothing. However, the Tlingit continued to sponsor their ancient ceremonies, particularly those associated with the memorial rites, and with it, the need for ceremonial objects and artisans to make them persisted.

Fortunately, the Tlingit artistic traditions survived through a few artists who had continued to manufacture objects for the ceremonies that had largely gone underground. The missionaries could support the production of Native art without its sinful attributes, and they actually encouraged the production of art for economic reasons to meet the demands of the tourist market. Some of the artists produced objects to meet the traditional, ceremonial needs as well as to sell in the tourist market. Generally, there was no comparison between the fine work produced for traditional use and the craft pieces made for the tourist market, which didn't meet the standards of traditional, ceremonial art.

Strangely, the economic depression of the 1930s also contributed to the survival of traditional art and the training of a core of new artisans. The government implemented a number of public work programs as a source of employment. One of the programs included the restoration of old totem poles that had been gathered from remote and abandoned village sites and brought to urban centers frequented by tourists. Additionally, new poles were made, which provided an opportunity for traditional artists to teach and mentor a cadre of young artists.

A number of young aspiring artists participated in arts programs that developed in Ketchikan and Haines during the 1960s or were introduced to Native arts through Indian studies programs in schools. A few fortunate students, such as the featured artist of these carving books, were able to study with Bill Holm, who is recognized for his study and knowledge of Northwest Coast art at the University of Washington. A few students were able to apprentice with senior master artists while others were self taught.

Within the last several years, Sealaska Heritage Institute (SHI) developed a series of projects to promote Native art, including its Native Artist Market, a Native art website, its Juried Art Show and Competition, Tlingit basketry weaving and carving classes, and design workshops. One of the institute's latest efforts is a series of books of "how to" carve. It is intended to be used alone or to supplement art classes. The text and photos demonstrate the successful integration of both traditional and modern tools and supplies. For example, the paint used by the artist derives from both ancient methods of making colors as well as from the commercial market.

Anthropologists, such as Sergei Kan, have suggested that the survival of Tlingit culture has its basis in its ceremonial life. Ceremonial objects are central to these activities, and thus artists play a vital role in our cultural survival. The persistence of Tlingit culture can also be attributed to our ability to adapt to social and economic change and our capacity to integrate our cultural values into the new institutional forms that affect our daily lives. The resilience and strength of Tlingit culture is clearly reflected in the ongoing production of sacred clan objects, and Tlingit adaptability is evident in the contemporary arts produced by Northwest Coast artists. The Tlingit overcame the historical oppressive acts to eradicate our culture, and our continued development and evolution is most apparent through our arts.

SHI applauds those artists who in the face of historical adversity continued the artistic tradition that gave the Tlingit, Haida, and Tsimshian international recognition and acclaim. SHI also thanks the editor, photographer, essay writer, and artist for their effort and contributions. We trust that future generations of artists will use these publications to guide them in their work. ◎

ROSITA WORL *(Yeidiklas'o_kw; _Kaa haní)*

Opening night of the 2008 Juried Art Show and Competition, a biennial event sponsored by Sealaska Heritage Institute. The goal is to perpetuate and enhance Tlingit, Haida, and Tsimshian art.

Introduction

The best way to learn how to carve Tlingit art is to apprentice with a master artisan or to enroll in workshops on Tlingit carving. One-on-one instruction is the most beneficial way to learn.

However, for many Native people this isn't possible. They may not have access to an accomplished carver in their villages, or they may have moved out of state but yearn to learn this ancient art tradition. This is the reason for this series of books on Tlingit carving.

The series was designed with an emphasis on clarity. Each step is paired with a color photograph to make it easier to follow than manuals that are only text based.

The series features three main projects on how to carve a tray, a hat, and a mask. I recommend starting with the book about trays, progressing to the hat project, and ending with the mask project. Even a beginner should be able to learn some basic techniques by completing the tray project.

Each book concludes with chapters on how to make traditional paint and paintbrushes, and how to inlay abalone and operculum into wood. Tlingit translations of names and words for projects are provided in italics.

Our ancestors produced astonishing works of art—masterpieces that rival works by the most renown artisans in the world. I hope in some small way this series will help to perpetuate the art of the Tlingit. ◎

Opposite: Southeast Alaska, the ancestral homeland of the Tlingit.

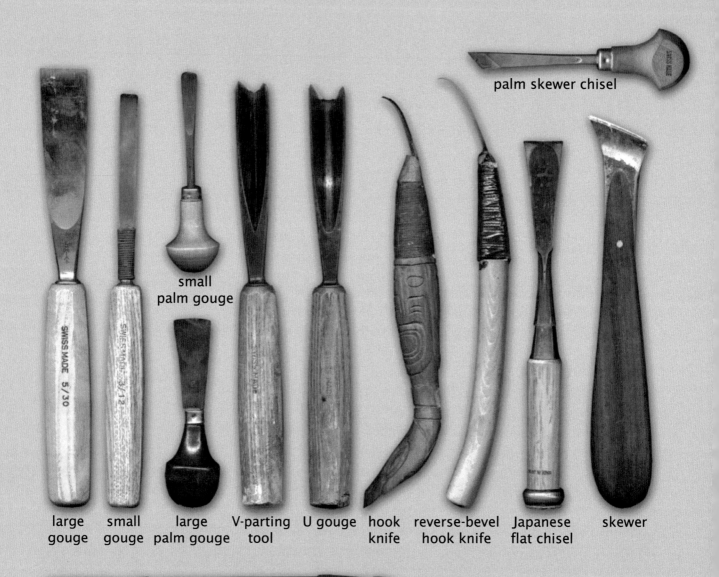

palm skewer chisel

large gouge

small gouge

large palm gouge

V-parting tool

U gouge

hook knife

reverse-bevel hook knife

Japanese flat chisel

skewer

small palm gouge

straight knife

small straight knife

Tlingit Tools *(Jishagóon)*

I own a large collection of tools, but I use only about six tools regularly. If I had to choose three tools, I would opt for a gouge, a straight knife, and an adze.

I purchase most of my tools from Woodcraft, a company with stores nationwide that also offers an online catalog.

I modify my blades to avoid making unwanted marks in my wood. For example, gouges come with sharp corners that leave cut marks in the wood. To avoid this, I grind the corners of my gouges until they are rounded.

Gouges come in many widths and shapes (some have deep sweeps while others have subtle sweeps). Generally speaking, large gouges with deeper sweeps will remove a greater amount of material. They are used for roughing out and for intermediate and finish work on carvings and sculptures of larger size. Small or narrow gouges generally are used for finish and detail cuts and for most work on smaller carvings.

V-parting tools are used to make V cuts. U gouges are used to recess large areas, cut troughs to outline shapes, and to make large V cuts.

Hook knives are used to cut cross grain and concave shapes and to hollow wood. The concave side of the blade is beveled. A reverse-bevel hook knife is similar to a hook knife but it is better at remov-

Opposite: A selection of tools from the author's collection.

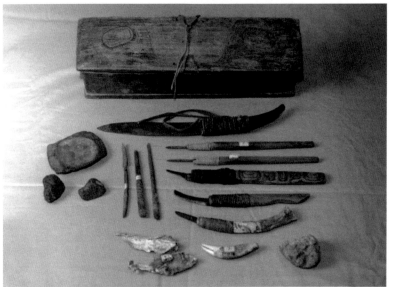

Man's lidded toolbox and contents, circa late nineteenth century. *Clockwise from top*: tool box, knife, two drills, three knives, pumice, a bear's tooth, dogfish skins, and paint supplies.

ing ridges from concave areas. The convex side of the blade is beveled.

Chisels are used to smooth flat surfaces, create corners in flat areas, trim edges, and make hair pegs.

Skewers are used to carve V cuts, remove high spots on convex shapes, and to remove wood.

Palm skewer chisels are used for intricate shaping and cutting fine details.

A straight knife is used to cut straight lines and V cuts, to remove high spots, and to trim edges. It works well when carving eyes and other two-dimensional work. Small straight knives are used for fine detail work.

A caliper is used to measure distance and thickness. Handheld calipers also are useful. A caliper also is known as a scribe.

A strop (leather) is used to sharpen blades. It's very important to always keep the blades sharp.

Mallets are used to pound blades into wood.

Flat pencils are used to make parallel lines at an equal distance from each other.

An adze is used to remove large amounts of wood and do rough shaping and finish work. It usually is used on rounded or flat surfaces. A lip adze is used to remove large amounts of wood from concave shapes, such as the back of a mask. When using an adze, hold your elbow against your side as you make cuts.◎

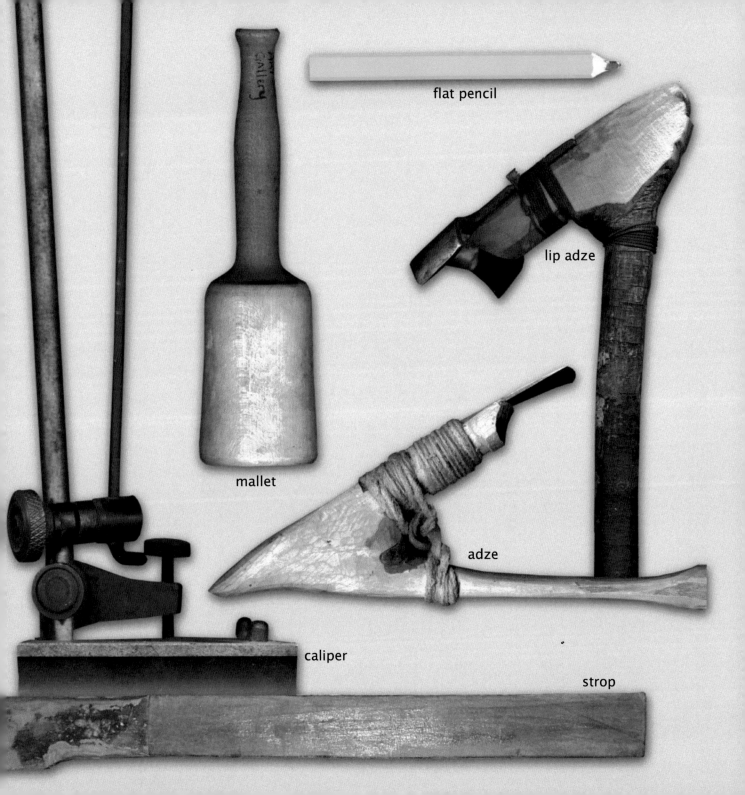

flat pencil

lip adze

mallet

adze

caliper

strop

Tlingit Dishes *(Kílaa)*

KATHY MILLER *(Teet Tláa)*

"Some of the most striking and aesthetically satisfying products of the Northwest Coast carvers' art are wooden bowls. Often without elaborate surface decoration, they depend on elegant proportion and relationships of pure form for their beauty."
—BILL HOLM

Traditional Northwest Coast wooden dishes are used primarily for holding and serving goods and food, and they usually are carved, inlaid, and/or painted to some degree with the owners' clan crests or spirit designs. Two of the most common forms of Tlingit dishes are bowls and trays.

Historically, bowls and trays were in daily use in homes, and the finest pieces were brought to the traditional feasts or ceremonies (ku.éex'). In this public setting, these larger and more elaborate pieces served as symbols of wealth and status of the clan owning them. It was at these events that "the hierarchy of dish sizes corresponded to the hierarchy of rank" (Jacknis 1973:17).

The species of wood used for Tlingit bowls varies, as should be expected from a culture that uses wood extensively, but non-resinous hardwoods such as alder, maple, and birch usually are chosen for the wooden bowls (Emmons 1991:160). They are carved from one solid piece of wood, and are never steamed and spread as are some other wooden containers. The resulting forms of wooden

Opposite: Tlingit tray to be carved in this project.

Tlingit bowl with carved designs on the ends. Inlaid with thirty-two opercula.

bowls range from rectangular and shallow with slightly bulging sides and a broad flange on the rim to oval or round bowls with high raised ends (Holm 1987:168, Holm 1973:28). "A universal characteristic of Northwest Coast bowl form is the undulating rim that is high at the ends and dips at the sides" (Holm 1984:72).

Frequently, the Tlingit bowl is carved in the form of an animal, including various insects and birds, beavers (Siebert and Forman 1967:36), sea otters, frogs, whales, and seals.

Long flat trays (see opposite page) are another type of wooden dish commonly used in the Northwest Coast culture, and they range in size from tiny miniatures to giant feast platters more than ten feet long. They also are made from one solid piece of hardwood and are never steamed or spread. Tlingit trays retain the basics of the overall wooden bowl form with broad flanges and upswept ends that are simply elongated, and subsequently create shallower, longer containers (Holm 1973:31, Holm 1984:75).

One of the famous photos taken circa 1885 by Winter and Pond in the Klukwan Whale House of the G̲aana̲xteidí Clan shows the clan's famous woodworm feast dish, which was more than seventeen feet long (John Marks, personal communication; photo in Emmons 1991:63 and in Holm and Reid 1975:21).

One way the long feast trays were used was for holding loads of berries; men would carry the berry-laden trays into a ceremony while singing their clan's entrance song (John Marks, personal communication). For more information on Tlingit ceremonies at which these trays and other wooden bowls were used, see Kan 1989, de Laguna 1972, and Emmons 1991.◎

This extraordinary Tlingit feast tray measures 59" long by 8" wide. A painted (but very faded) design inside the tray appears to be Northwest Coast formline. Opercula inlay. Artist unknown. Circa late 1800s. Sealaska Corporation Collection.

Tlingit Tray Project

In this project, I'll make a basic tray. Cut a green, hardwood log approximately 7" in diameter and 12" long. I am using alder, but you could also use maple, birch, or hemlock. Use a chainsaw or maul to cut the log in half lengthwise.

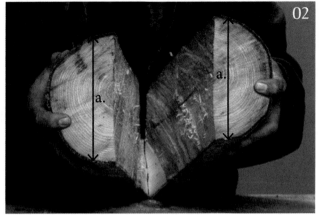

Using a saw, cut out and discard the heartwood (the dense wood in the center of the log) (a). You will be left with two pieces of wood that include bark. Choose the piece with the straightest grain and the fewest knots.

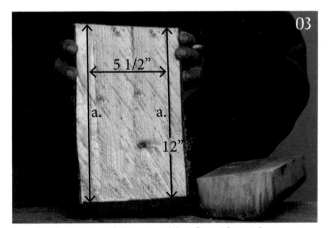

On the bottom of the tray (the flat side with no bark), draw two parallel lines lengthwise (a). The goal is to make the length at least twice as long as the wood is wide. In this case, the wood is 12" long, so the lines are drawn to create a width of 5 1/2".

Using an adze, remove the wood from the sides outside of the lines drawn in the previous step.

The next step is to make the bottom of the tray flat. Lay the wood (bark side up) on a flat surface. Using a flat pencil, draw a line on all sides around the bottom.

Rub the wood on a flat surface. This will discolor (and make visible) the raised portions of the wood that must be removed. A dirty garage floor is a good place to rub wood to expose the high spots.

If necessary, use a pencil to make the high spots exposed in the previous step more visible.

Using an adze, remove the high spots down to the pencil line drawn in step 5. Repeat steps 6–8 until the bottom is flat.

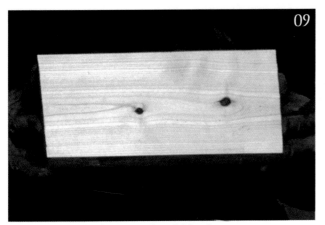

This is how the bottom should look.

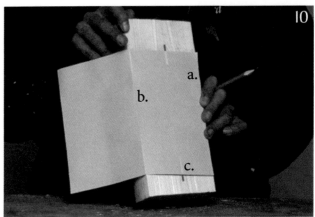

The next step is to create a centerline. On the bottom of the tray (side without bark), line up the edge of a piece of paper with the edge of the wood (a). Fold the paper over the other edge to create a crease (b). Fold the paper again, aligning the edge (a) with the crease (b). Make a mark on the wood where the second crease falls (c).

Use the paper or another straight edge to draw a centerline.

Continue the centerline on the ends of the wood. The centerline will be used for the entire project. It will not change. It's important to continually redraw your centerline as you remove wood.

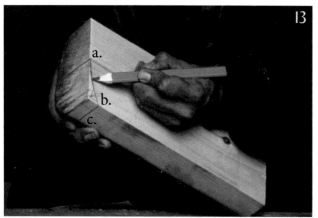

On the bottom, identify the lowest corner (the corner with the least amount of wood lengthwise). On the lowest corner, draw an arc from the centerline (a) to the edge (b). Continue the line on the side of the tray (c).

On the lowest corner, remove the wood outside the lines drawn in the previous step.

The next step is to make a template of that corner. Get the piece of paper you used before with a crease down the center. Align the crease (a) with the centerline (b). Push the end of the paper over the corner, creating a crease (c).

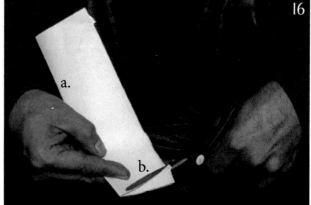

Draw an arc along the crease created in the previous step to make it more visible. Fold the paper along the centerline crease (a) and cut along the arc you just drew (b).

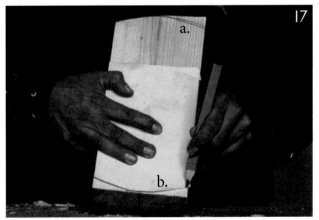

Unfold the paper and align one side of the curved end exactly on the corner you modified in step 14. Draw along the template on the other side of the wood (a). Draw the arc on the other end, too (b).

The next step is to draw lines on the sides from the bottom of the arcs (a) toward the bark. Do this on the other side, too (this is the same step as step 13 but for the remaining three corners).

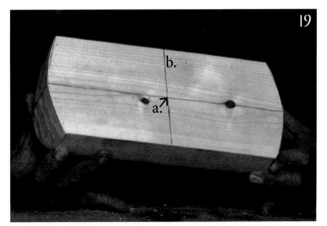

Using an adze, modify the other three corners the same way you modified the first corner. Also, using a measuring tape, find the middle of the centerline along the length of the wood (a). Draw another centerline through that point, establishing the centerline for the width (b).

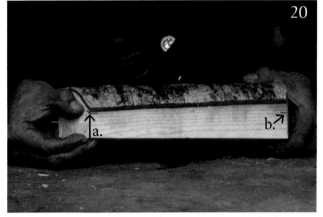

The next step is to determine the corner with the least amount of wood from bottom (a) to top. On that corner, draw a mark just below the bark. Make a mark establishing the height of this corner on the other corners, too (b).

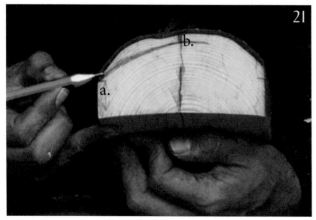

Draw an arc connecting the mark on the lowest corner (a) to the centerline on the end of the wood (b).

Using an adze, remove the wood above the arc on that corner.

The next step is to make a template of the corner you modified in the previous step. Align the edge of a piece of paper on the centerline on that end (a). Press the paper over the modified corner.

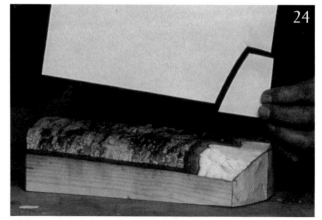

Draw along the crease to make it more visible and cut along the crease. You now have a template of that corner.

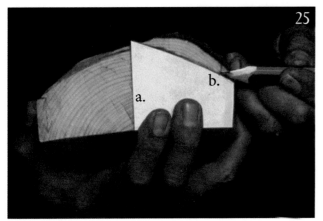

Align the edge of the template on the centerline of the modified end (a) and draw along the arc on the other side (b).

Repeat the previous step on the other end. Next, modify these three corners as you did in step 22, removing the wood above these new arcs. Make sure you remove the wood along the arc all the way down to the corners (a).

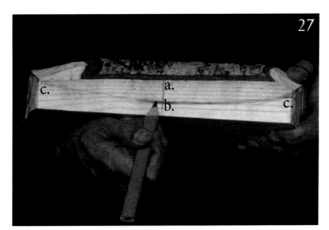

The next step is to establish the height of the sides. First, extend the centerline you drew in step 19 to the sides of the tray (a). Make a mark on the centerline approximately 1/2" from the bottom of the tray (b). Draw a curved line that connects this point to the corners (c). Repeat this step on the other side.

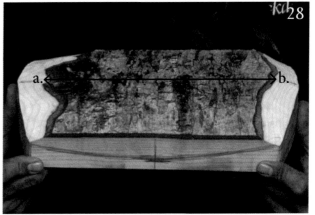

The next step is to begin removing wood from the top of the tray (between a and b).

Using an adze, start in the middle and work toward an end. Flip the wood around and repeat this step.

As you remove the bark, extend the centerline to the top of the tray.

Continue to remove wood from the top, working toward the sides, away from the centerline.

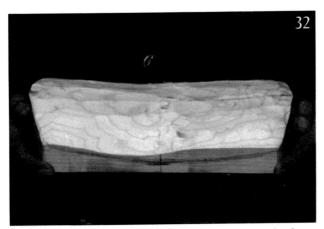

In this image, you can see the left side is roughed out. Continue removing wood until both sides match.

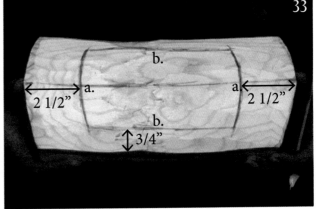

The next step is to draw a box on the top of the tray. On the final tray, the top of the ends will be convex (bulge outward) while the ends and sides on the bottom will be concave (curve inward). Also, the ends will be higher than the sides. And, the ends will be about three times wider than the sides. Draw a box 2 1/2" from the ends (a) and 3/4" from the sides (b). The ends of the box (a) should curve like the ends of the tray.

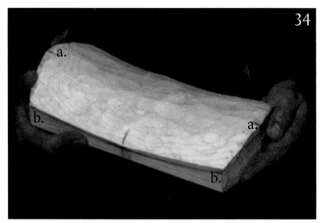

Remove more wood from the top. Notice how the ends are starting to slope and the ends (a) are much higher than the sides (b).

Redraw the box and remove any high spots inside the box.

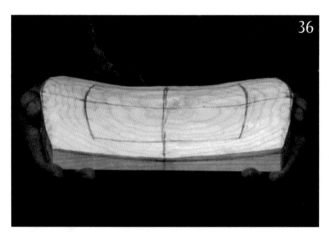

Redraw your centerlines.

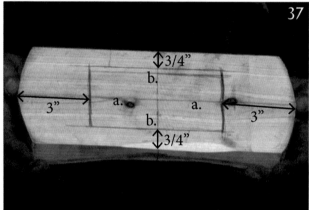

On the bottom, draw a box approximately 3" from the ends (a) and 3/4" from the sides (b). This box represents the foot of the tray.

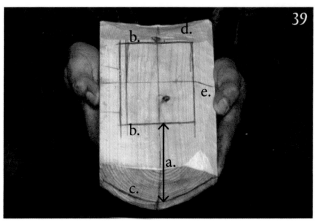

Draw an arc on the ends approximately 1/2" from the top of the tray (a).

The next step is to remove the wood from the bottom of the tray at each end (a). You'll remove wood at a slope from the ends of the box (b) to the arc you drew in the previous step (c). As you can see in this image, wood is already removed from the far end (d) and the right side (e).

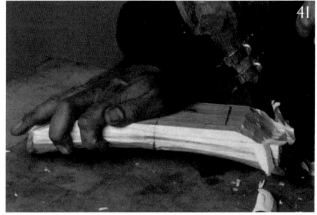

In progress.

In progress.

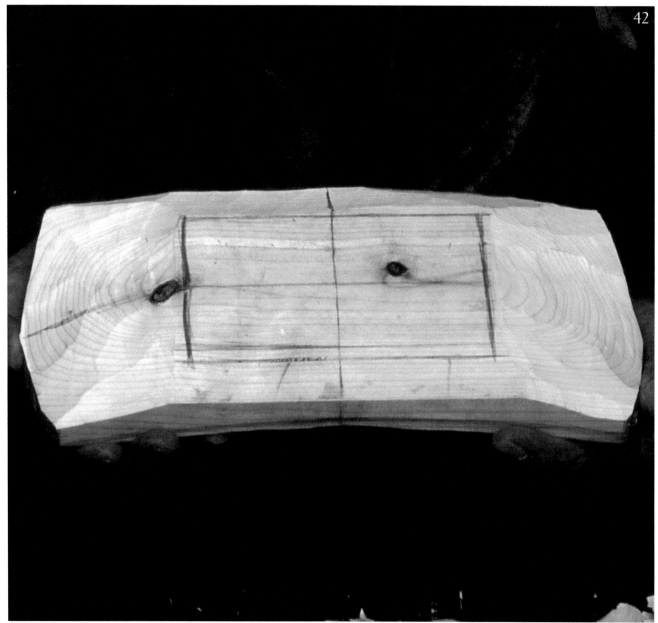

This is what the bottom should look like so far.

On the bottom, remove wood from the sides, using a hook knife. The sides will be concave (curve inward) on the final tray.

The next step is to refine the ends of the bottom. On the final tray, the sides and ends (on the bottom) will be concave. You must scoop out the wood to create a curve. In this image, you can see the far end is already scooped out. Use a hook knife.

In progress.

Further refine the sides to make them concave.

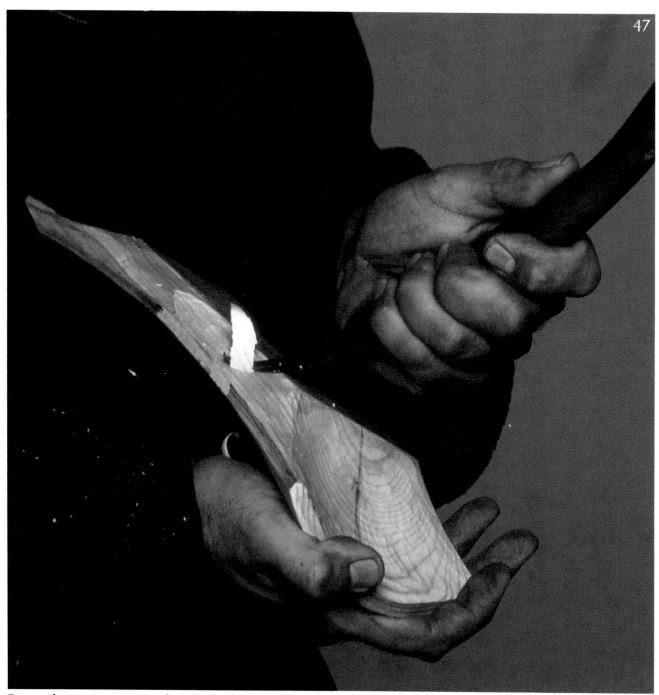

Repeat the previous step on the other side.

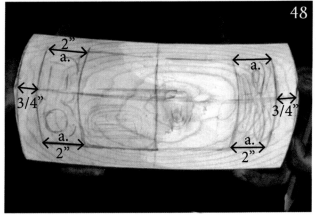

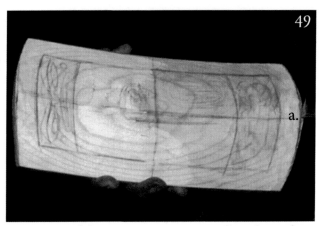

Notice the top now has the beginnings of a design. This project will not have such a design, but I did this to show where a design for a future tray should be placed. Extend the box on your tray to include the portion showing the design (a). The extension should be approximately 2" long and end 3/4" from the ends.

Determine if there is any excess wood on the ends. The ends should be a smooth arc. Draw an arc on each end and remove any wood outside the arcs (a).

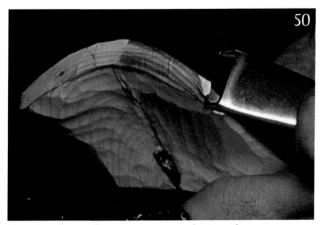

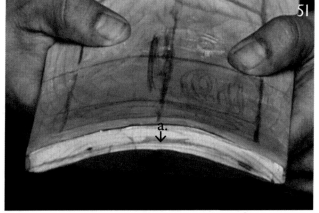

To trim the ends, use a gouge, placing the concave side of the blade on the wood. Work from the corners toward the centerline.

Draw arcs on each end approximately 1/4" from the top (a). You'll use this line as a guide. One of the last steps will be to refine the ends down to this line.

Shave the wood between the ends of the tray and the box on top, creating a slope.

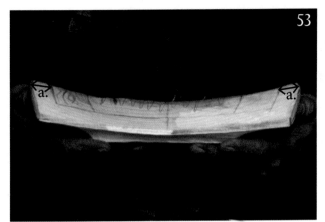

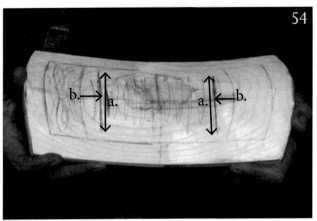

You should have achieved a subtle angle from the ends of the tray to the box (a).

The next step is to hollow out the top of the tray. Draw two vertical lines approximately 3/4" from the ends of the inner box (a). The scribbles visible between these lines indicate the area of the tray that must be removed to within 1/2" from the bottom. The new lines (a) represent the boundaries of the inner box. The inner walls will slope from the curved lines (b) to the new lines (a).

Using an adze, start cutting in the center.

Turn the wood continually at 90° to 180° angles.

Gently tease the wood out as you work toward the lines drawn in step 54.

58

Continue to remove wood until the interior is roughly hollowed out close to the lines. The next step is to cut in walls. You must build a little box in the center. This will be the deepest area.

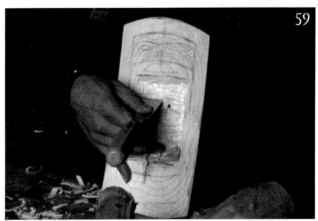

59

Using a gouge and mallet, gently cut in the walls of the inner box straight down to within 1/2" from the bottom. Do this all the way around until you have an inner box with crisp lines.

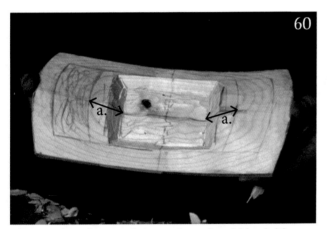

60

This is what the rough inner box should look like. The next step is to create slopes on the ends of the inner box (a).

61

Carve in the slopes using a gouge and mallet.

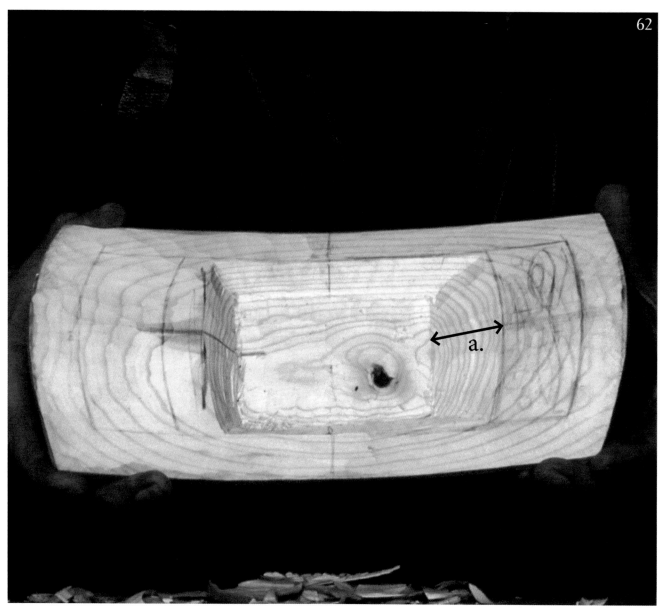

This is how the sloped end should look (a). Repeat the previous step on the other end.

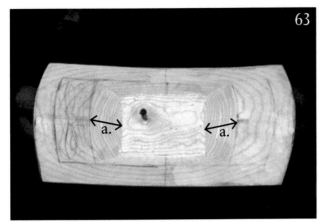

This is how the inner box should look with both ends sloped (a).

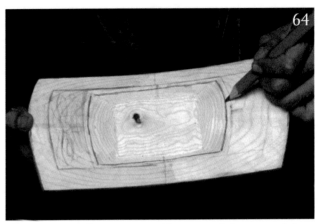

The next step is to create a lip around the top of the inner box. Draw a line approximately 1/4" from the top edge all the way around.

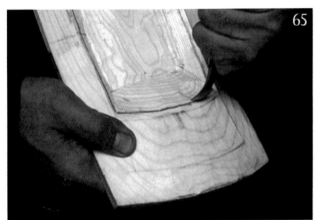

Using a small, curved gouge, remove a bit of wood under the line drawn in the previous step (this is called undercutting). Do this all the way around inside the inner box until you have created a lip.

Use a hook knife to gouge out the area beneath the lip. The area under the lip should be concave.

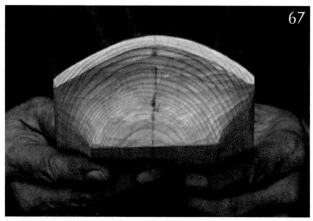

Smooth out the entire tray, refining the ends down to the arcs drawn in step 51.

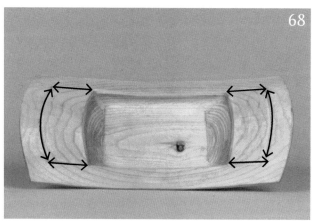

Make a cut along the lines on the top of the tray.

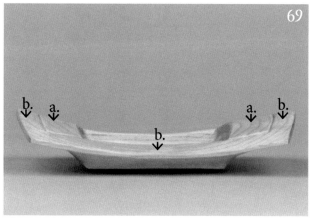

This is a basic tray. As you get more advanced, you may want to embellish your trays with carved designs and inlays. The designs would be carved on the top of the tray (a). Inlays, such as opercula and abalone, would be recessed on the edges (b). ◎

Tlingit Paint *(Néegwál')*

KATHY MILLER *(Teet Tláa)*

At the time of European contact in the late 1700s, painted designs were found all along the Northwest Coast on numerous items, including house fronts, boxes, totem poles, masks, hats, and rattles (Gilbert and Clark 2000:69; Duff 1974).

Quite a range of colors was available in these traditional, pre-contact paints, from white to various reds and yellows, with the principal colors being red, black, greenish blue, yellow and white (de Laguna 1972:415–416). The pigments were made from fungus, moss, lichen, berries, charcoal, cinnabar, lignite, salmonberry leaves, iron fillings, copper, and red and brown ochre (Bolanz and Williams 2003:133; Emmons 1991:447; Holm 1965:26).

The primary sources had to be prepared to achieve the desired hue. For example, alder or hemlock bark was boiled in urine to obtain a true red color; other shades of red were made from hematite, fungus, or red ochre; black was made from charred alder; white was made from burnt clamshells; blue-green was made from green earth; and mustard yellow was made from another ochre (Stewart 1973:70; Emmons 1991:198, 449; Gunther 1966:11–12).

The pigments were then mixed with specific binding agents, depending on the ultimate use of the paints. For example, if the paint were intended for use on objects, then the pigment was mixed with the glutinous part of salmon eggs, as this mixture helped the paint

Opposite: Richard Beasley crushing rock used to make green-blue paint. It is sometimes referred to as totemic green.

33

This Tlingit war helmet from the late eighteenth century likely has its original paint. It was sold to a private collector at auction in 2008 for $2,185,000, the highest amount of money ever paid for a Native American item at auction.

withstand the elements (Stewart 1973:70; McLennan 2000:97). A gloss finish was added to black paint by the addition of graphite into the pigment mix (Gilbert and Clark 2000:69).

The physical sources of the paint materials were highly valued resources to the Tlingit people, and the pigment varieties were identifiable as being from different locations and were highly valued trade items. Just as certain clans and houses held ownership rights and defended other valuable resources, such as subsistence areas, they also would protect the sources of paint pigments (McLennan 2000:97).

By the late nineteenth century, commercially prepared paints from Europe were available in more colors and in brighter colors, and were in use by artists on the Northwest Coast. A brilliant blue paint was already in use by 1830 (McLennan 2000:97; Holm 1984:44). The new paints withstood exposure to the elements and fading better than did the traditional paints, but nonetheless many artists continued to use the more traditional, softer hues of traditional paints (Gunther 1966:11–12).

Within the overall context of Northwest Coast art, the painting helps to amplify the two- and three-dimensional forms (Gilbert and Clark 2000:69). "In the use of color we find one of the great unifying characteristics of the art" (Holm 1965:25).

On a side note, colors in the Tlingit language are named after things that occur in the natural environment. For example, red (*gagaan kas'úkwxu yáx yatee*) translates to "the sky at sunset" and yellow (*tl'áatl' yáx yatee*) is "the color of yellow warbler" (Paul 1944:18). ◎

Top left, clockwise: Green earth (any rock rich in copper deposits) is used to make green paint, bark is one source used to make red paint, salmon eggs are used to bind pigment, and charred wood is used to make black paint.

Tlingit Paint *(Néegwál')* 35

Tlingit Paint Project

01

02

In this project you'll learn to make green-blue and red paint. Place a chunk of azurite or other rock high in copper, such as malachite, on a grinding stone or other hard surface. Using a pick, chip off the colored crystals, hitting them at a sideways angle. The crystals are made more brittle when hit from the side, making them easier to pulverize.

Crush the material with another rock, grinding the crystals as finely as possible. The rock you use to grind must be harder than the mineral; use a rock such as basalt. Grind the crystals into a coarse powder.

03

04

To further refine the powder, put it on a sheet of glass and add drops of water until the powder is wet but not runny. Place another sheet of glass over it and rub in a circular motion until the material is the consistency of toothpaste. Remove the glass and let the mixture dry at room temperature until the water evaporates, leaving a silt-like powder.

Place dog salmon eggs on the grinding rock, then add the dry powder. The quantity of salmon eggs should be approximately double the volume of powder. For example, if you have one teaspoon of powder, add two teaspoons of eggs. Grind materials with a second rock until well mixed. Add a drop or two of water as needed.

05

Dip a paintbrush into the mixture and stroke to test color intensity. If it is too pale, add more pigment. If it is too intense, add more eggs or water (one drop at a time). Once the desired color is achieved, use the paint immediately. Make only the quantity you need—it will not keep. It will dry within an hour and become unusable.

To make red paint, get a chunk of red fungus known as Indian Red. This fungus is found on dead hemlock trees and presents itself in bumps on the trunk. Knock off a few chunks of fungus and roast them at 400° for one to two hours. The roasting will intensify the color. File the fungus to remove the pigment. This fungus is very hard and the process requires time and perseverance.

Use a toothbrush to transfer any excess fungus from the file to a board.

Separate the yolk from the white of one chicken egg. Beat the yolk (you can use dog salmon eggs instead of a chicken yolk).

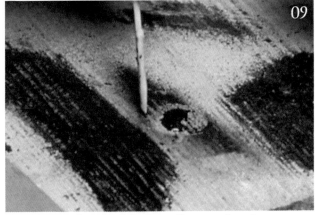

Using a toothpick, dab the yolk onto the pigment and mix until the desired color is achieved.

Color will vary depending on the age and quality of the fungus. Use this paint immediately. It will harden within an hour and become unusable.◎

Tlingit Paintbrushes *(Kooxéedaa)*

KATHY MILLER *(Teet Tláa)*

Paintbrushes of various sizes are used by Northwest Coast artists for painting two- and three-dimensional objects. Traditionally, Tlingit paintbrushes were made out of porcupine quills or animal guard hairs that were set into wood handles (Stewart 1973:71; Gilbert and Clark 2000:69). The porcupine quills or hairs were placed in the handle to project 1/4" to 1/2", and then the paintbrush was wrapped with split spruce root or sinew to keep the bristles in place in the handle (Emmons 1991:196–197). The bristles were then cut off to form an angled tip on the usable end.

The handles can be rounded and slim, which allows for easier rotation in the painter's hand (Holm 1965:28). An artist may have had a dozen or more paintbrushes of various sizes, and sometimes the handles of the larger paintbrushes were intricately carved with the artist's crest designs (Emmons 1991:197; Gunther 1966:11–12).

Commercially made paintbrushes were in use along the Northwest Coast by the mid-nineteenth century (Gilbert and Clark 2000:69), and carvers today use a wide variety of commercial brushes with synthetic and natural bristles. In the early 1900s, a house screen in the Yakutat Shangukeidí Thunderbird House was painted, in part, with a special paintbrush. The artist, a Ĺuknax̱.ádi man, incorporated his son's fingernails into the construction of one of his paintbrushes. This was done "in order to transfer to the child some of his artistic skill" (de Laguna 1972:326–327). ◎

Opposite: Tlingit paintbrushes to be made in this project.

Tlingit Paintbrush Project

Find a tree that was snapped in two by wind. Trees snapped by wind will produce shards or spikes at the breaking point on the trunk. You will use a shard of wood for the paintbrush handle. Select a few shards. If the shards are not green, soak them in water overnight before you begin. Using a saw, cut a shard to approximately 1' long.

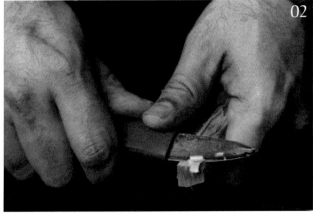

Determine the thickest end of the shard. This end will be the tip (the end with the bristles). Using a knife, square the tip, shaving the wood until the tip is a rectangle approximately 3/4" wide by 1/4" high (tip dimensions of brushes vary depending on the size of brush sought by the artist).

Starting from the tip, shave the wood on the handle, tapering the handle so it's thinner than the tip.

In progress.

The next step is to cut a slit in the tip to hold the bristles. First, tightly wrap approximately two feet of string around the wood two inches from the end of the tip. The pressure exerted by the string will stop the blade from cutting through the entire length of the shard.

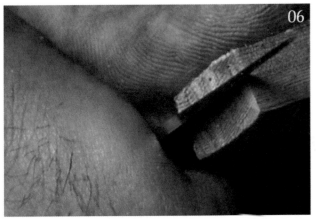

Place the edge of the blade on the center of the tip. It's important to position the blade along the grain lines and not across them. Gently apply pressure on the blade, moving it back and forth to tease the wood apart. Once the wood cracks back to your stop string, remove the blade.

The next step is to create a collar and taper the tip. Draw a taper line from one corner of the tip to approximately 1/2" from the tip (a). Draw a collar line approximately 1/2" from the end of the tip all the way around (b). Using a straight knife, make a slight cut along the collar line (b).

Shave the wood toward the cut you made along the collar line to create a slight indentation. The cut you made in the previous step will stop the blade at the collar line. Apply very little pressure and be very gentle.

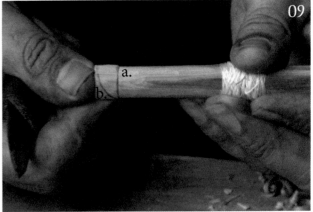

This is what your paintbrush should look like with the ridge carved around the collar. The ridge (a) will keep the binding from sliding off of the tip. Next, remove the wood outside of the taper line (b).

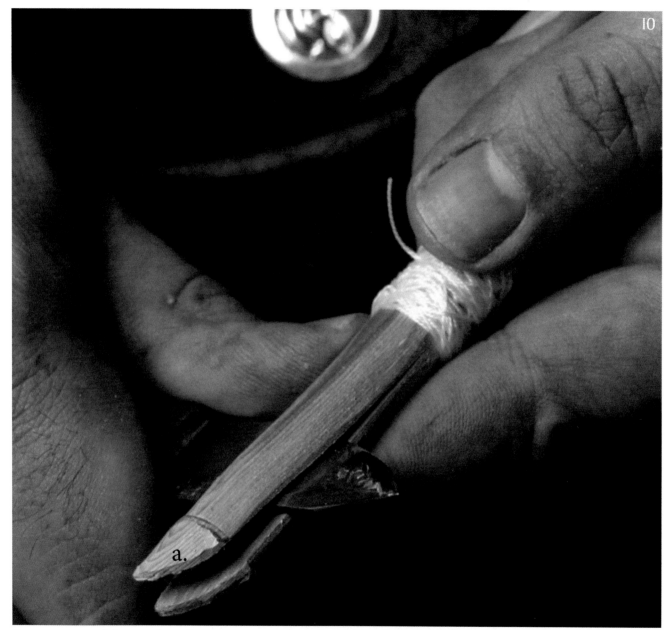

Remove some of the wood on the tip, creating a slope from the collar line to the tip (a).

The next step is to create the bristle bundle. From a pile of porcupine quills, separate the guard hairs. Guard hairs are distinct from quills and other hairs because they are very long and rough.

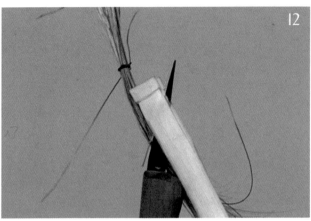

Group the guard hairs into a bundle approximately half the thickness of the paintbrush tip. Group the hair ends that were in the porcupine's body together (these ends are distinctive because they are sharp). Use a guard hair to bind the bundle approximately 1 1/2" from the sharp ends.

Gently open the tip with a blade. Insert the bundle of hair with the sharp ends oriented inside the handle. Make sure you situate the tie directly under the lower lip of the collar (a). By putting the tightest-bound section of hair here, you minimize the risk of loose hairs sticking out the sides of the tip. Stuff the rest of the bundle into the handle.

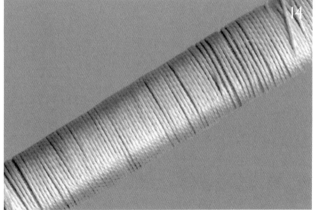

Cut approximately two yards of string. Remove the existing string from the handle. Begin binding by starting near the tip (right below the collar line) and working toward the handle. Tightly wrap the handle (the string will want to slide down the handle but by securing it tightly at the bottom, it will prevent it from unraveling).

When you get to the end of the split, tie a knot, bury the knot in the string, and cut the string ends. Trim the ends of the bristles to approximately 1/2" long. Cut the bristles at a diagonal. ◎

Tlingit Inlay *(Anaxh awliteen)*

KATHY MILLER *(Teet Tláa)*

A common way to embellish valuable carved items on the North-west Coast is by inlaying additional materials such as teeth and shells into the wood. Art historians have studied the possible progression of use of the various materials for inlaying in Northwest Coast art by reviewing the records of early explorers and by viewing older items in museum collections. The use of sea-otter teeth and the opercula of sea snails seems to predate the use of abalone shell, as exhibited by the fact that these two materials were observed by the earliest voyagers to the Northwest Coast (Drucker 1948:395). Opercula and abalone are two of the most common materials used for inlay today.

Opercula (singular: operculum) are part of the shells of sea snails that are oval in shape and white or ivory in color with some tan spots. The operculum (Latin for "little lid") is a corneous plate at the opening of the shell, attached dorsally to the foot of the snail. This fingernail-like structure seals the aperture, serving as a cover against predators when the snail body is retracted. It also enables the snail to survive periods of drought.

Traditionally, operculum was obtained by the Tlingit of South-east Alaska from the Natives of Vancouver Island through trade. It commonly was used as inlay detail for masks, armor collars, food dishes, chests, and other carvings, and was very often used to repre-

Opposite: Abalone inlay in wood.

sent teeth (Emmons 1991:174; Wardwell 1996; Collins, et.al. 1973).

Abalone is an edible mollusk whose shell has an iridescent, blue-green lining. The species of abalone native to the Northwest Coast is the northern abalone, but the southern sub-species is more colorful. The local Alaska shell is comparatively very pale in color with a thinner, more friable shell, and therefore had less value (Emmons 1991:174). The more colorful abalone shell is found along the West Coast only up to Monterey Bay, and therefore had to be traded for by the Tlingit with Native Americans from California. This increased its value and significance when it was used (Davis 1949:19).

The Natives of the Northwest Coast say that abalone was already in use before contact with white men, and traditionally, heated spruce gum was used to affix the abalone to the objects (Emmons 1991:174). Northern abalone is now a protected species, and most abalone used today is imported from New Zealand (Shearer 2000:15).

Dentalia are ocean mollusks whose shells were obtained through trade from the Nootka and Quatsino Kwakwaka'wakw (formerly known as Kwakuitl) of Vancouver Island. They also were used to embellish Northwest Coast objects, but more frequently they were attached to blankets and tunics that were worn as regalia, rather than inlaid into carved wooden items (Emmons 1991:173–174). The Tlingit did not use dentalia as frequently as many other Northwest Coast tribes.

The Raven House of the Lukaax̱.ádi Clan House in Haines, Alaska, had two rows of opercula inlaid around the outside of the front door, one indication that they were a very wealthy clan (John Marks, personal communication). The *Two Door House* Chilkat Robe still owned by this clan shows this operculum inlay in its woven design (Dauenhauer and Dauenhauer 1994:230). A famous mosquito mask collected by Captain Edward G. Fast in 1867 in Southeast Alaska has more than seventy opercula in its mouth as teeth (Harvard Peabody Museum Accession #69–30–10/1607, Wardwell 1996:153). ◎

Opposite: Owl and Humpback Shakee.át by Richard A. Beasley (Deex̱wudu.oo). This piece with multiple abalone inlay won first place at the 2002 Juried Art Show and Competition sponsored by Sealaska Heritage Institute.

Tlingit Inlay *(Anaxh awliteen)* 51

Tlingit Inlay Project

In this project you'll learn how to inlay opercula and two techniques to inlay abalone. Starting with opercula, lay a shell on the wood and draw around it.

Using a small gouge, remove a bit of wood inside the circle you drew around the operculum.

Place the operculum over the circle, seating the bottom edge of the shell on the bottom edge of the circle. Press the top edge of the operculum onto the circle and draw a line along that edge. Remove the wood between that line and the circle.

Repeat step 03 until the operculum seats snugly in the wood. As the wood dries, it will tighten around the operculum.

05

There are two ways to inlay abalone. Usually you will cut your wood first, and then trim your abalone to fit the cut. However, if you have a piece of pre-cut abalone, you'll need to reverse the process. Take your pre-cut abalone and draw around it onto your wood. Make sure the inner surface of the abalone is the side exposed.

Using a small gouge, remove a bit of wood inside the circle.

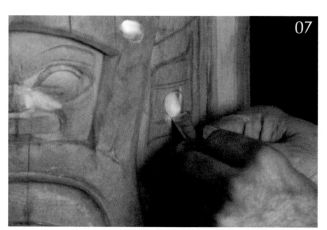

It helps to cut around the circle first, and then gouge out the wood inside the cut.

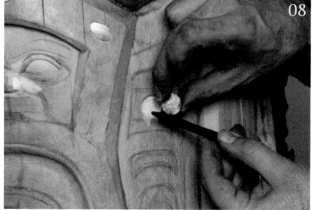

Rub the edges of the abalone on a stick of charcoal. Whenever possible, pre-drill holes in the wood all the way through so the abalone can be poked out with a toothpick in case it gets stuck.

Place the abalone in the hole and move it around. The charcoal will rub off and expose wood around the hole that must be removed. Remove the wood with a small gouge. Place the abalone back in the hole and draw around any edges that are protruding. Remove wood on these lines. You may need to repeat this step several times before the abalone fits into the hole.

Brush rubber cement onto a block of wood and the back of a piece of Wet-Dry sandpaper. When the cement dries, slap the sticky sides of the wood and sandpaper together.

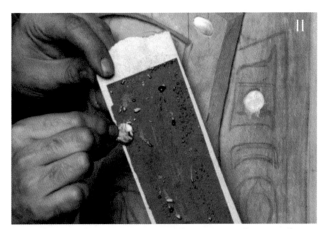

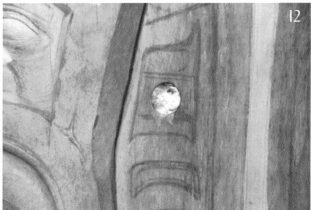

Wet the sandpaper. You now have a sanding stick. Rub the underside of the edge on the sandpaper, grinding in a bevel. This will make it easier to seat the abalone. Important! Use liquid on the sandpaper during this process to prevent inhalation of abalone spores, which cause lung disease.

Place the abalone in the hole to test the fit. The abalone should fit snugly but not perfectly. It's better to leave one side slightly higher, rather than flush with the wood. This will make light play more dramatically on the shell.

The second technique for inlaying abalone is more common. First, draw the shape you want your abalone to assume. In this case, we're doing an eye. Using a small gouge, remove the wood inside the eye.

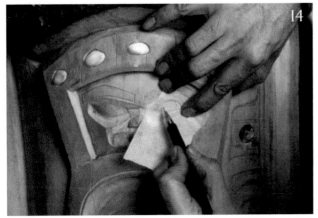

The next step is to create a template. Put a piece of paper over the eye hole and draw the shape onto the paper.

Cut out the hole. You now have a template of the shape. Lay the paper circle on a piece of abalone and draw around the paper onto the shell.

Cut the abalone to shape while holding it under running water. Use sandpaper to refine the shape.

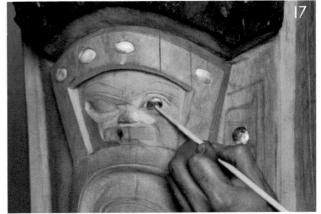

Place the abalone on the hole. Seat one section of the abalone where you want it. In this case, we are seating the upper portion of the shell. Sand whatever portions of the shell do not fit.

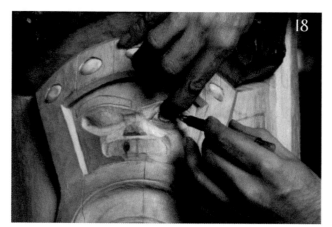

You may need to cut off a sliver of wood to seat the abalone snugly. To do this, draw around any area where the abalone falls outside the hole. Enlarge the hole to that line.

As the wood dries, it will shrink and tighten around the abalone. For this reason, you must recess the hole so the abalone doesn't pop out when the wood shrinks. ◎

References

Bolanz, Maria and Gloria C. Williams
    2003. *Totem Poles and Art of the Alaskan Indians*. Surrey: Hancock House.

Collins, Henry B., Frederica de Laguna, Edmund Carpenter and Peter Stone
    1973. *The Far North: 2000 Years of American Eskimo and Indian Art*. Washington, D.C.: National Gallery of Art.

Dauenhauer, Nora and Richard
    1994. *Haa Kusteeyí, Our Culture: Tlingit Life Stories*. Seattle: University of Washington Press; Juneau: Sealaska Heritage Foundation.

de Laguna, Frederica
    1972. *Under Mt. St Elias: The History and Culture of the Yakutat Tlingit*. Washington D.C.: Bureau of American Ethnology.

Drucker, Phillip
    1948. "The Antiquity of the Northwest Coast Totem Pole." In *Journal of the Washington Academy of Science*, vol. 38, no. 12, pp. 389–397.

Duff, Wilson with Bill Holm and Bill Reid
    1974. *Arts of the Raven: Masterworks by the Northwest Coast Indian*. Exhibit Catalogue, The Vancouver Art Gallery 15 June–24 September 1967. Vancouver: Vancouver Art Gallery.

Emmons, George T.
    1991. *The Tlingit Indians*. Seattle: University of Washington Press. New York: American Museum of Natural History.

Gilbert, Jim, and Karin Clark
    2000. *Learning By Designing. Pacific Northwest Coast Native Indian Art*. Vol. 2. Vancouver: Hemlock Printers Ltd.

Gunther, Erna
    1966. *Art in the Life of the Northwest Coast Indians*. Portland: Portland Art Museum.

Holm, Bill

    1965. *Northwest Coast Indian Art: An Analysis of Form*. Seattle: University of Washington Press.

    1973. "Structure and Design." In *Boxes and Bowls Decorated Containers by Nineteenth Century Haida, Tlingit, Bella Bella, and Tsimshian Indian Artists*. Smithsonian Institution and National Museum of the American Indian Washington and London: Smithsonian Press.

    1984. *The Box of Daylight: Northwest Coast Indian Art*. Exhibition Catalog, Seattle Art Museum. Seattle: University of Washington Press.

    1987. *Spirit and Ancestor*. Seattle and London: University of Washington Press.

Holm, Bill and William Reid

    1975. *Form and Freedom: A Dialogue on Northwest Coast Indian Art*. Houston: Institute for the Arts, Rice University.

Jacknis, Ira S.

    1973. "Functions of the Containers." In *Boxes and Bowls Decorated Containers by Nineteenth Century Haida, Tlingit, Bella Bella, and Tsimshian Indian Artists*. Smithsonian Institution and National Museum of the American Indian Washington and London: Smithsonian Press.

Kan, Sergei

    1989. *Symbolic Immortality: The Tlingit Potlatch of the Nineteenth Century*. Washington and London: Smithsonian Institution Press.

Keithahn, Edward L.

    1962. "Human Hair in Tlingit Art." In *Alaska Sportsman,* May 1962.

Marks, John

    2007. Personal communications with Kathy Miller.

McLennan, Bill

    2000. *The Transforming Image: Painted Arts of the Northwest Coast First Nations*. Vancouver: University of British Columbia Press.

Paul, Frances

    1944. *Spruce Root Basketry of the Alaska Tlingit*. Lawrence: Haskell Institute.

Shearer, Cheryl

    2000. *Understanding Northwest Coast Art*. Seattle: University of Washington Press.

Siebert, Erna and Werner Forman

    1967. *North American Indian Art: Masks, Amulets, Wood Carvings and Ceremonial Dress from the Northwest Coast*. London: Paul Hamlyn Ltd.

Stewart, Hilary

1973. *Stone, Bone, Antler, and Shell Artifacts of the Northwest Coast*. Seattle: University of Washington Press.

Wardwell, Allen

1996. *Tangible Visions: Northwest Coast Shamanism and Its Art*. New York: The Monacelli Press.

About the Contributors

Richard A. Beasley *(Deexwudu.oo)* is a Raven *(Yéil)* of the Coho *(L'uknax.ádi)* Clan. He is a lifelong carver who has worked as a professional artist for nearly thirty years. He apprenticed under Steve Brown, Duane Pasco, Loren White, and the famed Tlingit carver Nathan Jackson. He also took classes from renowned Northwest Coast art expert Bill Holm, professor emeritus of art history and anthropology at the University of Washington, where Beasley earned a bachelor's degree in metal design.

Kathy Miller *(Teet Tláa)* is a Raven *(Yéil)* who was adopted into the Coho Salmon *(L'uknax.ádi)* Clan. She has worked within the Tlingit culture of Southeast Alaska for many years. She holds a master's degree in cultural anthropology from Colorado State University. She is the executive director of the Huna Heritage Foundation.

Rosita Worl *(Yeidiklas'okw; Kaa haní)* is an Eagle *(Ch'áak')* of the Thunderbird *(Shangukweidí)* Clan. She holds a doctorate in anthropology from Harvard University and wrote her doctoral dissertation on Tlingit property law. She is the president of Sealaska Heritage Institute.

Mark Kelley is one of Alaska's most published photographers. He has created and published a series of books, calendars, note cards, and postcards over the years. He has lived in Alaska for more than thirty years and resides in Juneau.

Opposite: Legend of the Raven and the Whale silkscreen by Richard A. Beasley (Deexwudu.oo). An illustration of a story owned by the Coho (L'uknax.ádi) Clan.

Made in the USA
Las Vegas, NV
12 November 2023